The Rip in the Hat

By Debbie Croft

Tim sat in the pit.

Mits can nap.

Nap at the mat, Mits.

Tim can see his hat.

His hat is at the tap.

Tim ran!

Mits ran to the hat.

Mits bit the hat.

Mits rips the hat!

Tim ran to his hat.

Mits sat.

CHECKING FOR MEANING

1. Where did Tim's hat blow off? *(Literal)*

2. Who ripped the hat? *(Literal)*

3. Why do you think Mits ripped the hat? *(Inferential)*

EXTENDING VOCABULARY

nap	What does the word *nap* mean? Look at the letters. Can you make another word from the word *nap*?
hat	Look at the word *hat*. Which sound is changed to turn *hat* into *cat*?
rip	Look at the word *rip*. What sounds are in this word?

MOVING BEYOND THE TEXT

1. How do you think Tim felt when he saw that his hat had ripped?

2. What would you do if you were Tim in this situation?

3. How do you think Mits might feel after ripping Tim's hat?

SPEED SOUNDS

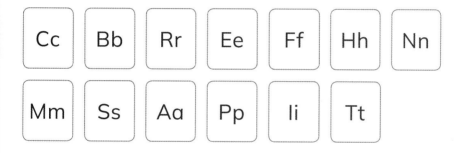

| Cc | Bb | Rr | Ee | Ff | Hh | Nn |
| Mm | Ss | Aa | Pp | Ii | Tt |

PRACTICE WORDS

in

nap

can

Nap

hat

ran

bit

rips

rip

Rip